From House Hunter To Landlord

The Complete Handbook for Property Investment

Benjamin Phillips

From House Hunter to Landlord:
The Complete Handbook for Property Investment in 2024

Dedicated to my loving wife, Laura.
You are my everything and without you, we wouldn't be where we are today. Thank you for keeping me grounded.

Table Of Contents

Chapter 1: Introduction to Property Investment

Why Invest in Single-Family Home Rental Properties?

If you are an investor, house hunter, flipper, landlord, or property manager, you may be wondering why investing in single-family home rental properties is a smart move. This subchapter will provide you with the answers you seek and shed light on the benefits of this particular niche in property investment.

Stability and Consistency
One of the primary reasons to invest in single-family home rental properties is the stability and consistency they offer. Unlike other types of properties, such as commercial or multi-family units, single-family homes tend to attract long-term tenants. Families and individuals often prefer the privacy and space that a single-family home provides, making it more likely for them to stay for an extended period. This stability allows you to enjoy consistent rental income and reduces the risk of frequent vacancies.

Lower Risk and Higher Returns

Investing in single-family homes also comes with lower risks and higher returns compared to other types of properties. The initial investment required is often more affordable, allowing investors to enter the market without a significant financial burden. Additionally, the demand for single-family homes is always present, regardless of economic conditions. This ensures a steady stream of potential tenants and minimizes the risk of prolonged vacancies.

Flexibility and Control

Owning single-family rental properties provides you with a level of flexibility and control that is not always possible with other types of investments. You have the freedom to choose the location, size, and features of the property based on your target market. This control allows you to tailor your investment strategy and cater to the specific needs of your tenants. Furthermore, managing a single-family home is often less complex than dealing with multi-unit properties, making it an ideal option for those new to property investment.

Appreciation and Wealth Building
Another attractive aspect of investing in single-family home rental properties is their potential for appreciation and wealth building. Over time, the value of real estate tends to increase, allowing you to build equity and wealth. By owning multiple single-family homes, you can leverage this appreciation to expand your portfolio and increase your rental income. This gradual accumulation of assets can lead to significant financial rewards in the long run.

In conclusion, investing in single-family home rental properties offers stability, consistency, lower risk, higher returns, flexibility, control, and the potential for wealth building. Whether you are a seasoned investor or just starting your journey in property investment, this niche provides an excellent opportunity to generate passive income and secure your financial future.

Understanding the Benefits and Risks of Property Investment

From House Hunter to Landlord:
The Complete Handbook for Property Investment in 2024

Investing in single-family home rental properties can be an excellent way to build wealth and create a steady stream of passive income. However, like any investment, there are both benefits and risks that need to be carefully considered before diving into the world of property investment. In this chapter, we will explore the various advantages and potential pitfalls associated with this type of investment, providing valuable insights for investors, house hunters, flippers, landlords, and property managers alike.

One of the primary benefits of investing in single-family home rental properties is the potential for long-term appreciation. Historically, real estate has proven to be a reliable asset class that tends to increase in value over time. By purchasing a well-located property in an area with strong market fundamentals, investors can benefit from capital appreciation and build equity in their investment.

In addition to appreciation, rental income is another key advantage of property investment. Single-family homes typically offer higher rental yields compared to multi-unit properties, making them an attractive choice for investors. With proper research and due diligence, investors can identify properties that generate consistent rental income, providing a reliable cash flow stream.

Furthermore, property investment allows for diversification of investment portfolios. By adding real estate to their asset mix, investors can reduce overall portfolio risk and potentially achieve higher returns. Real estate often exhibits lower volatility compared to other investment options, making it an appealing option for those seeking stability in their investment strategy.

However, it is essential to acknowledge and understand the risks associated with property investment. Market fluctuations, economic downturns, and unexpected repair costs are some of the potential pitfalls that investors may face. It is crucial to conduct thorough market research, analyze property cash flows, and have contingency plans in place to mitigate these risks effectively.

Additionally, being a landlord or property manager comes with its own set of challenges. Dealing with tenant issues, maintenance requests, and legal obligations can be time-consuming and stressful. It is essential for landlords and property managers to have a strong understanding of local rental laws and regulations to protect their investments and ensure compliance.

In conclusion, property investment offers numerous benefits, including potential appreciation, rental income, and diversification. However, it is crucial to approach this investment strategy with caution and a thorough understanding of the risks involved. By conducting due diligence, creating a solid investment plan, and staying informed about market trends, investors, house hunters, flippers, landlords, and property managers can navigate the world of single-family home rental property investment successfully.

Setting Realistic Goals and Expectations

When it comes to single-family home rental property investment, it is crucial for investors, house hunters, flippers, landlords, and property managers to set realistic goals and expectations. This subchapter delves into the importance of establishing achievable targets and managing expectations in the dynamic world of property investment.

One of the first steps in setting realistic goals is to conduct thorough research and analysis. Investors must understand the local market trends, rental demand, and property values in the area they are targeting. By gathering this information, they can assess the feasibility of their investment goals and make informed decisions.

It is essential to define specific and measurable goals. Whether it's acquiring a certain number of properties within a timeframe, achieving a target rental income, or increasing property value through renovations, having concrete objectives allows investors to track their progress and make necessary adjustments along the way.

While it is important to aim high, it is equally crucial to remain realistic. Investors should consider factors such as their financial capabilities, market conditions, and time constraints when setting goals. Unrealistic goals can lead to disappointment and frustration, which may discourage investors from further pursuing their investment journey.

Managing expectations is equally vital in the property investment niche. Investors must understand that property values may fluctuate, rental demand may vary, and unexpected challenges may arise. By setting realistic expectations, investors can better prepare themselves for potential setbacks and develop strategies to mitigate risks.

Additionally, it is crucial to have a long-term perspective when setting goals and managing expectations. Property investment is not a get-rich-quick scheme; it requires patience and dedication. Investors should be prepared for the ups and downs of the market and understand that their goals may take time to achieve.

To ensure the achievement of realistic goals, investors should develop a comprehensive investment plan. This plan should outline the steps to be taken, the resources required, and a timeline for achieving the desired outcomes. Regularly reviewing and updating this plan will help investors stay on track and adapt to changing circumstances.

In conclusion, setting realistic goals and expectations is vital for success in single-family home rental property investment. By conducting thorough research, defining specific objectives, managing expectations, and developing a comprehensive investment plan, investors can navigate the property market with confidence and increase their chances of achieving long-term success.

Overview of the Book's Structure and Content

From House Hunter to Landlord: The Complete Handbook for Property Investment is a comprehensive guide that caters to a diverse audience of investors, house hunters, flippers, landlords, and property managers. Specifically targeted towards those interested in single-family home rental property investment, this book offers valuable insights and practical advice on navigating the world of real estate investment.

From House Hunter to Landlord:
The Complete Handbook for Property Investment in 2024

The book begins by providing a brief introduction to the booming real estate market and its potential for long-term financial growth. It emphasizes the importance of understanding the fundamentals of property investment and lays the foundation for readers to build their knowledge and expertise.

To ensure a solid understanding of the subject matter, the book follows a logical structure, divided into several key sections. It starts with a thorough explanation of the different types of investment properties available, highlighting the benefits and drawbacks of single-family homes. Readers will gain insight into the market trends and factors to consider when evaluating potential investment opportunities.

The next section delves into the process of house hunting, offering practical tips and strategies for finding and analyzing properties. It covers essential topics such as location selection, property inspections, and assessing market value. Readers will also learn about negotiating deals, conducting due diligence, and navigating financing options.

Once an investment property has been acquired, the book shifts focus to the role of a landlord. It provides guidance on managing tenants, including rental agreements, tenant screening, and property maintenance. Readers will also gain invaluable tips for ensuring a steady rental income, handling tenant disputes, and maximizing property value through effective property management strategies.

Finally, the book concludes with a discussion on the potential for expanding a rental property portfolio and venturing into other real estate investment opportunities. It explores the benefits of diversifying investments and shares insights on strategies such as house flipping, short-term rentals, and property development.

Written in an accessible and engaging manner, From House Hunter to Landlord: The Complete Handbook for Property Investment offers a wealth of knowledge to investors, house hunters, flippers, landlords, and property managers looking to succeed in the world of single-family home rental property investment. Whether you are a beginner in the field or an experienced investor, this book is your go-to resource for mastering the art of property investment and maximizing your returns.

Chapter 2: Preparing for Property Investment

Assessing Your Financial Situation and Budgeting for Investments

As an investor, house hunter, flipper, landlord, or property manager in the niche of single-family home rental property investment, it is crucial to have a clear understanding of your financial situation and effectively budget for your investments. This subchapter will guide you through the essential steps of assessing your financial health and developing a robust budgeting strategy to maximize your returns and minimize risks.

Before diving into the world of property investment, it is essential to evaluate your current financial situation. Start by assessing your income, including your monthly salary, additional sources of revenue, and any potential passive income streams. Calculate your monthly expenses and identify areas where you can potentially cut costs to allocate more funds towards investments. Understanding your financial standing is crucial as it will help determine the amount of capital you can allocate towards property investments.

Once you have a clear picture of your financial situation, it is time to develop a budgeting strategy for your investments. Begin by setting realistic goals and defining your investment objectives. Are you looking for long-term rental income or short-term flipping opportunities? This will help you determine the type and location of properties you should consider.

Next, create a comprehensive budget that encompasses all the costs associated with property investment. This includes the purchase price, closing costs, property taxes, insurance, maintenance, repairs, and property management fees, among others. Make sure to factor in potential vacancies and the cost of marketing and tenant acquisition.

Consider working with a financial advisor or a real estate investment expert to ensure your budget is realistic and aligned with your long-term goals. They can provide valuable insights into the local market, rental demand, and projected returns on investment.

Regularly review and update your budget as market conditions and your financial situation change. Keep track of your income, expenses, and return on investment to assess the profitability of your properties and make informed decisions for future investments.

Remember, successful property investment requires careful financial planning and disciplined budgeting. By assessing your financial situation and creating a comprehensive budget, you will be well-equipped to navigate the world of single-family home rental property investment and achieve long-term financial success.

Evaluating Your Risk Tolerance and Investment Strategy

From House Hunter to Landlord:
The Complete Handbook for Property Investment in 2024

When it comes to venturing into the world of property investment, understanding your risk tolerance and developing a sound investment strategy is crucial. This subchapter will guide you through the process of evaluating your risk tolerance and help you craft an investment strategy tailored to your goals as an investor, house hunter, flipper, landlord, or property manager in the niche of single-family home rental property investment.

Firstly, let's delve into risk tolerance. Every investor has a unique comfort level when it comes to taking risks. Some individuals are more conservative and prefer lower-risk investments, while others are willing to embrace higher-risk opportunities for potentially higher returns. It's essential to assess your risk appetite realistically and honestly before making any investment decisions.

To determine your risk tolerance, consider factors such as your financial stability, investment goals, time horizon, and personal circumstances. Ask yourself questions like: How much capital can I afford to lose without significant financial implications? Am I looking for steady long-term income or short-term gains? Do I have the time and expertise to actively manage my investments? By understanding your risk tolerance, you can align your investment strategy accordingly.

Next, developing an investment strategy is vital for success in the single-family home rental property market. Start by setting clear objectives, such as cash flow generation, property appreciation, or portfolio diversification. Identify the specific types of properties that align with your goals and evaluate the potential risks and rewards associated with each.

Consider factors like location, property condition, rental demand, and local market trends. Conduct thorough research, consult with experienced investors or professionals, and leverage tools such as market analysis reports to make informed decisions. Additionally, explore financing options, tax implications, and property management strategies that best suit your investment strategy.

Remember that an effective investment strategy requires periodic reviews and adjustments. The real estate market is dynamic, and economic conditions can change rapidly. Stay informed about market trends, maintain a diversified portfolio, and adapt your strategy as needed to maximize returns and minimize risks.

In conclusion, evaluating your risk tolerance and developing an investment strategy are crucial steps for success in the single-family home rental property niche. By understanding your risk appetite, setting clear objectives, conducting thorough research, and staying informed, you can make informed investment decisions that align with your goals and aspirations as an investor, house hunter, flipper, landlord, or property manager.

Building a Strong Credit Profile and Maintaining Good Financial Health

In the world of property investment, having a strong credit profile and maintaining good financial health is essential for success. Whether you are an investor, house hunter, flipper, landlord, or property manager, understanding the importance of credit and financial stability is crucial in achieving your goals within the niche of single-family home rental property investment.

First and foremost, building a strong credit profile is the foundation of any successful investment journey. Lenders and financial institutions rely heavily on credit scores to assess your creditworthiness and determine the terms and conditions of any loans or financing you may require. Therefore, it is imperative to establish and maintain a good credit history by paying your bills on time, keeping credit card balances low, and avoiding excessive debt.

To start building your credit profile, obtain a copy of your credit report from the major credit bureaus and review it for any errors or discrepancies. If you identify any inaccuracies, promptly dispute them and work towards their resolution. Additionally, consider opening a few lines of credit, such as credit cards or small loans, to demonstrate your ability to manage debt responsibly.

Maintaining good financial health goes hand in hand with building a strong credit profile. It involves adopting prudent financial habits that will not only benefit your property investment endeavors but also your overall financial well-being. Start by creating a budget and sticking to it. This will help you track your income, expenses, and savings, ensuring that you have a clear understanding of your financial situation.

In addition to budgeting, it is crucial to establish an emergency fund. This fund should consist of three to six months' worth of living expenses, providing a safety net in case of unexpected financial challenges. By having an emergency fund, you can navigate any unforeseen circumstances without jeopardizing your property investments or accumulating unnecessary debt.

Furthermore, regularly reviewing and managing your debts is crucial for maintaining good financial health. Keep track of your debt-to-income ratio and aim to keep it at a manageable level. Pay off high-interest debts first and consider consolidating multiple debts into a single loan with a lower interest rate, if beneficial.

In conclusion, building a strong credit profile and maintaining good financial health are essential components of successful single-family home rental property investment. By establishing a positive credit history, managing your finances responsibly, and adopting prudent financial habits, you are setting yourself up for long-term success in the property investment industry. Remember, good credit and financial health not only open doors to better financing options but also provide stability and security in your investment journey.

Establishing Relationships with Lenders and Real Estate Professionals

In the world of single-family home rental property investment, establishing solid relationships with lenders and real estate professionals can be the key to success. Whether you are an investor, house hunter, flipper, landlord, or property manager, understanding the importance of these relationships is crucial for your long-term success in the industry.

Lenders play a vital role in property investment. They provide the financial backbone that allows you to acquire properties and expand your portfolio. It is essential to establish relationships with lenders who specialize in real estate investment and understand the unique needs of this niche. These professionals can help you navigate the complex world of financing, ensuring that you secure the most favorable terms and rates for your investments. Building trust and rapport with lenders will also increase the likelihood of obtaining funding for future projects.

Real estate professionals, such as agents and brokers, are another essential part of your network. These individuals possess valuable knowledge of the local market and can help you find the best investment opportunities. By developing relationships with real estate professionals, you gain access to off-market deals, exclusive listings, and valuable insights into emerging neighborhoods. They can also assist in negotiating favorable purchase prices and guide you through the purchasing process.

Networking and attending industry events are excellent ways to connect with lenders and real estate professionals. Local real estate investment associations, conferences, and meetups provide opportunities to meet like-minded professionals and build relationships. Additionally, leveraging online platforms and social media can help you connect with experts and stay informed about the latest trends and opportunities in the market.

Remember, relationships are a two-way street. While lenders and real estate professionals can offer invaluable support, it is crucial to demonstrate your professionalism and commitment to your investment goals. Be responsive, reliable, and respectful of their time and expertise. Maintaining open lines of communication and nurturing these relationships will be mutually beneficial in the long run.

In conclusion, establishing strong relationships with lenders and real estate professionals is essential for anyone involved in single-family home rental property investment. By cultivating these relationships, you gain access to financing options, market insights, and valuable resources that can propel your investment journey forward. Invest time and effort into building and maintaining these connections, and you will reap the rewards in your property investment endeavors.

Chapter 3: Finding Profitable Investment Opportunities

Researching and Analyzing Local Real Estate Markets

From House Hunter to Landlord:
The Complete Handbook for Property Investment in 2024

One of the most critical aspects of successful single-family home rental property investment is thoroughly researching and analyzing local real estate markets. Whether you are an investor, house hunter, flipper, landlord, or property manager, understanding the dynamics of the market you are operating in is key to making informed decisions and maximizing your profits.

To begin your research, it is essential to gather data on various factors that can influence the local real estate market. This includes demographics, employment rates, population growth, average income levels, and crime rates. Analyzing these factors will provide you with a comprehensive overview of the area's economic stability and potential demand for rental properties.

Additionally, studying market trends and historical data is crucial in identifying patterns and predicting future market performance. Analyze the average home prices, rental rates, and occupancy rates in the area over the past few years to determine if the market is on an upward trajectory. Understanding the cyclical nature of real estate markets can help you time your investments strategically.

Another vital aspect of researching local real estate markets is studying the competition. Identify other rental properties in the area and analyze their amenities, rental rates, and tenant satisfaction. This will help you gauge the demand and competition in the market and allow you to position your property effectively to attract tenants.

Furthermore, it is essential to stay updated with local zoning laws, regulations, and any upcoming developments or infrastructure projects that may impact the market. Changes in zoning laws can restrict or expand your property's potential use, while new developments can significantly influence property values and rental demand. Being aware of these factors will help you make informed decisions and adapt your investment strategy accordingly.

When analyzing a local real estate market, it is crucial to consider both the short-term and long-term prospects. While a market might be thriving currently, it is essential to assess its sustainability and potential for growth in the future. Look for indicators such as job growth, new businesses moving into the area, and planned infrastructure projects to gauge the market's long-term viability.

In conclusion, researching and analyzing local real estate markets is a fundamental step for anyone involved in single-family home rental property investment. By gathering and analyzing data on demographics, market trends, competition, and local regulations, you can make informed decisions and position yourself for success in your investment endeavors. Stay proactive in monitoring market changes and adjust your strategy accordingly to maximize your profits and achieve long-term success as an investor, house hunter, flipper, landlord, or property manager.

Identifying Neighborhoods with High Rental Demand and Low Vacancy Rates

Subchapter: Identifying Neighborhoods with High Rental Demand and Low Vacancy Rates

As an investor, house hunter, flipper, landlord, or property manager focused on single-family home rental property investment, one of the most crucial aspects of your success lies in identifying neighborhoods with high rental demand and low vacancy rates. This subchapter aims to equip you with the essential knowledge and strategies to make informed decisions when choosing the right location for your rental properties.

Understanding the dynamics of rental demand and vacancy rates is vital in ensuring a consistent cash flow and maximizing returns on your investment. By targeting neighborhoods with high rental demand, you can attract a steady stream of potential tenants, reducing the likelihood of extended vacancies and ensuring a constant influx of rental income.

From House Hunter to Landlord:
The Complete Handbook for Property Investment in 2024

To begin with, it is crucial to conduct thorough market research. Look for areas experiencing population growth, economic development, and job opportunities. These factors directly influence rental demand as individuals and families seek accommodation in proximity to their workplaces and amenities. Analyzing local economic indicators, such as employment rates and industry diversification, can provide valuable insights into the stability and growth potential of a neighborhood.

Furthermore, consider the demographic profile of the area. Are there universities or colleges nearby? Is it a family-friendly community with good schools and parks? Understanding the target market for your rental property will help you tailor your investment to the needs and preferences of potential tenants, increasing your chances of attracting and retaining high-quality renters.

Another important aspect to consider is the vacancy rate within a neighborhood. Low vacancy rates indicate a high demand for rental properties, reducing the risk of having your property sitting empty for extended periods. Research local housing market reports and vacancy rate statistics to identify areas with consistently low vacancy rates. Additionally, drive around the neighborhood to assess the overall condition of properties, as well-maintained properties often attract responsible tenants and contribute to lower vacancy rates.

Utilizing online platforms and real estate databases can be invaluable in your search for neighborhoods with high rental demand and low vacancy rates. These resources provide access to rental market analytics, historical data, and market forecasts, enabling you to make data-driven decisions.

By identifying neighborhoods with high rental demand and low vacancy rates, you position yourself for long-term success as a property investor, house hunter, flipper, landlord, or property manager. Investing in areas with a strong rental market ensures a consistent cash flow, minimizes vacancies, and maximizes your return on investment. Remember, thorough market research, understanding local economic indicators, and assessing demographic profiles are key steps to identifying the most lucrative neighborhoods for your rental properties.

Understanding Property Appreciation and Growth Potential

In the world of real estate investment, one of the most important factors that every investor, house hunter, flipper, landlord, and property manager should understand is property appreciation and growth potential. This subchapter aims to provide a comprehensive understanding of these concepts, particularly in the context of single-family home rental property investment.

From House Hunter to Landlord:
The Complete Handbook for Property Investment in 2024

Property appreciation refers to the increase in the value of a property over time. It is a crucial aspect for any investor as it directly influences the return on investment. Understanding the factors that contribute to property appreciation can help make informed decisions and maximize profits. These factors include location, market trends, economic conditions, infrastructure development, and demand for housing.

Location plays a vital role in property appreciation. Investing in a property located in an area with high growth potential, such as proximity to schools, shopping centers, employment hubs, and transportation facilities, can significantly impact its value over time. Additionally, understanding market trends and economic conditions can help investors identify areas with high appreciation rates and avoid potential pitfalls.

Furthermore, infrastructure development is a key driver for property appreciation. Areas witnessing significant infrastructure projects, such as new highways, airports, or commercial centers, often experience a surge in property values. Investors who stay informed about such developments can seize opportunities for substantial growth potential.

Another crucial factor in property appreciation is the demand for housing. Understanding the demographics and the rental market in a specific area is essential. Areas with a growing population, high employment rates, and a shortage of housing are likely to experience higher demand, leading to increased property values.

It is important to note that property appreciation is not solely reliant on external factors. As an investor, house hunter, flipper, landlord, or property manager, you can also play an active role in enhancing the growth potential of a property. This can be achieved through renovations, improvements, and effective property management strategies. Upgrading a property with modern amenities, maintaining it properly, and providing exceptional tenant experiences can contribute significantly to its appreciation.

In summary, understanding property appreciation and growth potential is paramount for anyone involved in single-family home rental property investment. By considering factors such as location, market trends, economic conditions, infrastructure development, and demand for housing, investors can make informed decisions and maximize their returns. Additionally, actively improving and managing the property can further enhance its growth potential. With this knowledge, you can navigate the real estate market with confidence and achieve long-term success in your investment endeavors.

Utilizing Online Listings, Real Estate Agents, and Networking for Property Leads

In the world of single-family home rental property investment, finding the perfect property to add to your portfolio can sometimes feel like searching for a needle in a haystack. With so many options and factors to consider, it's crucial to have a comprehensive strategy in place to ensure you're making the most informed decisions. In this subchapter, we will explore the power of utilizing online listings, real estate agents, and networking to uncover valuable property leads.

1. Online Listings: The digital age has revolutionized the way we search for properties. Online listings platforms, such as Zillow, Realtor.com, and LoopNet, provide a wealth of information at your fingertips. These platforms allow you to narrow down your search based on location, price range, and other specific criteria. By regularly monitoring these listings, you can stay up-to-date on the latest properties available in your target areas.

2. Real Estate Agents: Partnering with experienced real estate agents can be a game-changer in your property investment journey. These professionals have extensive knowledge of the local market and access to exclusive listings that may not be available to the general public. They can provide valuable insights, negotiate on your behalf, and help you navigate the complex process of purchasing a property. Building relationships with reliable real estate agents can give you a competitive edge when it comes to finding the best deals.

3. Networking: Networking is a powerful tool in any industry, and property investment is no exception. Attend local real estate events, join investment clubs, and participate in online forums to connect with like-minded individuals, industry experts, and potential sellers. By expanding your network, you increase your chances of finding off-market deals or receiving insider information about upcoming properties. Don't underestimate the power of personal connections in the world of property investment.

By combining the resources offered by online listings, the expertise of real estate agents, and the opportunities provided through networking, you can enhance your property lead generation efforts. Remember to stay proactive and dedicated to your search, as the best opportunities often require persistence and a keen eye for potential. As an investor, house hunter, flipper, landlord, or property manager, these strategies will help you uncover hidden gems and make sound investment decisions that align with your goals.

In conclusion, the process of property investment involves more than just luck. By utilizing online listings, real estate agents, and networking, you can increase your chances of finding the perfect single-family home rental property to add to your portfolio. Embrace these strategies, adapt them to your unique circumstances, and watch your property investment journey flourish.

Chapter 4: Conducting Due Diligence on Potential Investments

Evaluating Property Condition and Potential Renovation Costs

From House Hunter to Landlord:
The Complete Handbook for Property Investment in 2024

When it comes to investing in single-family home rental properties, one of the key factors to consider is the property's condition and the potential renovation costs involved. This subchapter will guide investors, house hunters, flippers, landlords, and property managers on how to effectively evaluate property condition and estimate renovation costs, ensuring that you make informed decisions and maximize your return on investment.

Before making any purchase, it is essential to conduct a thorough property inspection. This should include a detailed examination of the structural integrity, electrical and plumbing systems, roof, and overall condition of the property. Hiring a professional inspector is highly recommended, as they can provide an unbiased assessment and identify any potential issues that may require renovation or repair.

Once you have assessed the property's condition, it's time to estimate the potential renovation costs. Start by creating a comprehensive list of all necessary repairs and improvements. This may include cosmetic updates such as painting, flooring, and landscaping, as well as major renovations like kitchen and bathroom remodeling or replacing outdated HVAC systems.

To accurately estimate renovation costs, consider obtaining multiple quotes from licensed contractors or specialists in each area of renovation. Don't forget to factor in additional expenses like permits, materials, and labor costs. It is crucial to have a realistic understanding of the potential costs involved to avoid unexpected financial burdens down the line.

As an investor or landlord, it is essential to strike a balance between the property's condition and the renovation costs. While you want the property to be in good condition to attract tenants, you also need to ensure that the renovation costs do not exceed your budget or the potential return on investment.

To assist in evaluating property condition and potential renovation costs, utilize online resources and software specifically designed for property investors. These tools can provide insights into average renovation costs in your area and help you make more informed decisions.

Remember, successful property investment is all about finding the right balance between property condition, renovation costs, and potential rental income. By thoroughly evaluating the property's condition and estimating renovation costs, you can make informed decisions and ensure that your investment is a profitable one.

In conclusion, evaluating property condition and potential renovation costs is a crucial step in the process of investing in single-family home rental properties. By conducting thorough inspections, obtaining multiple quotes, and utilizing online resources, investors, house hunters, flippers, landlords, and property managers can make informed decisions and maximize their return on investment.

Assessing Rental Income Potential and Cash Flow Analysis

One of the most critical aspects of property investment, particularly in the niche of single-family home rental properties, is assessing the rental income potential and conducting a comprehensive cash flow analysis. This subchapter aims to equip investors, house hunters, flippers, landlords, and property managers with the necessary knowledge and tools to make informed decisions regarding rental properties.

When considering a potential rental property, it is essential to evaluate its rental income potential. This involves researching the local rental market, analyzing rental rates for similar properties in the area, and understanding the demand for rental homes. Understanding the rental income potential will provide you with a realistic expectation of the revenue you can generate from the property and help you determine whether it aligns with your investment goals.

Once you have determined the rental income potential, conducting a cash flow analysis becomes crucial. This analysis involves assessing all income and expenses associated with the property to determine its profitability. Income sources include monthly rental income, additional fees, and potential tax benefits. On the other hand, expenses may include mortgage payments, property taxes, insurance, maintenance costs, and property management fees.

A thorough cash flow analysis will enable you to calculate the property's net operating income (NOI), which is the income generated after deducting all expenses. This figure is vital in determining the property's cash flow and whether it will be a profitable investment. Positive cash flow indicates that the property generates more income than expenses, while negative cash flow suggests potential financial challenges.

Furthermore, it is crucial to account for unexpected expenses and vacancies when conducting a cash flow analysis. Setting aside a portion of the rental income for maintenance and repairs will ensure that you are adequately prepared for any unforeseen costs that may arise. Additionally, factoring in potential vacancies will help you assess the property's resilience during periods of non-occupancy.

By thoroughly assessing the rental income potential and conducting a cash flow analysis, investors, house hunters, flippers, landlords, and property managers can make informed decisions and maximize their returns. Understanding the local rental market, accurately calculating expenses, and accounting for potential vacancies will provide a solid foundation for successful property investment. Remember, it is essential to regularly reassess the rental income potential and conduct updated cash flow analyses to ensure that your investment remains profitable and aligned with your goals.

Reviewing Title Documents, Zoning Regulations, and Property History

When it comes to investing in single-family home rental properties, it is crucial to conduct thorough research and due diligence before making any purchase. This subchapter will guide you through the process of reviewing title documents, zoning regulations, and property history to ensure a smooth and successful investment journey.

Title documents play a significant role in property transactions as they establish ownership rights and any potential encumbrances. As an investor, it is essential to examine the title documents carefully to verify the property's legal status and identify any existing liens or claims that may affect your investment. By conducting a title search or hiring a professional title company, you can obtain a comprehensive report that outlines the property's ownership history, any outstanding mortgages or judgments, and easements or restrictions that may impact the property's use.

Understanding zoning regulations is vital for any property investment. Zoning laws dictate how a property can be used, such as residential, commercial, or mixed-use, and can influence its value and potential rental income. By reviewing the local zoning regulations, you can ensure that your investment aligns with the intended use and avoid any legal complications or restrictions down the line. It is crucial to know if the property is zoned for residential purposes and if there are any proposed changes or upcoming developments in the area that may impact its marketability.

Delving into the property's history can uncover valuable insights that may impact your decision-making process. By researching the property's past sales records, you can assess its appreciation potential and gauge market trends in the area. Additionally, reviewing the property's maintenance records and any previous inspection reports can give you an idea of potential repair costs and ongoing maintenance requirements that may affect your budget.

Moreover, exploring the neighborhood's history, including crime rates, school districts, and nearby amenities, can help you assess the property's desirability and attractiveness to potential tenants. This information can influence your rental pricing strategy and market positioning.

In conclusion, reviewing title documents, zoning regulations, and property history is crucial for any investor, house hunter, flipper, landlord, or property manager involved in single-family home rental property investment. By conducting thorough research and due diligence, you can mitigate risks, make informed decisions, and maximize your return on investment. Remember, knowledge is power in the world of real estate, and by arming yourself with the right information, you can set yourself up for success in the property investment market.

Conducting Home Inspections and Assessing the Property's Long-Term Viability

One crucial step in the process of property investment, particularly in the niche of single-family home rental properties, is conducting thorough home inspections and assessing the property's long-term viability. Whether you are an investor, house hunter, flipper, landlord, or property manager, this subchapter aims to equip you with the necessary knowledge and skills to make informed decisions and ensure the profitability and success of your investment.

Home inspections are a vital component of the due diligence process when considering a property for investment. They involve a comprehensive examination of the property's physical condition, structural integrity, and overall functionality. Engaging a professional home inspector with experience in single-family homes is highly recommended to conduct a thorough evaluation.

During the inspection, the inspector will assess various aspects of the property, including the roof, foundation, electrical and plumbing systems, HVAC, and overall safety features. Additionally, they will identify any potential red flags such as water damage, mold, pest infestations, or structural issues that may require costly repairs down the line.

From House Hunter to Landlord:
The Complete Handbook for Property Investment in 2024

Assessing the property's long-term viability goes beyond the initial inspection. It involves evaluating factors that can impact its desirability and profitability over an extended period. Considerations may include the location's potential for growth, proximity to amenities, schools, transportation, and the overall market conditions.

Furthermore, it is essential to gauge the property's rental potential by researching the local rental market, understanding rental rates, vacancy rates, and tenant demand. Evaluating the property's potential for appreciation and its ability to generate positive cash flow is crucial to ensuring a lucrative investment.

In addition to the physical and financial aspects, assessing the property's long-term viability also involves considering its suitability to your investment goals and long-term strategy. For instance, if you are focused on long-term buy-and-hold investments, you may prioritize properties with stable neighborhoods, low tenant turnover, and minimal maintenance requirements.

Overall, conducting home inspections and assessing the property's long-term viability is a critical step in the property investment journey. It helps investors, house hunters, flippers, landlords, and property managers make informed decisions, mitigate risks, and optimize returns. By thoroughly evaluating the property's physical condition, rental potential, and long-term outlook, you can position yourself for success in the world of single-family home rental property investment.

Chapter 5: Financing Your Property Investments

Exploring Mortgage Options for Investment Properties

When it comes to investing in single-family home rental properties, understanding your mortgage options is crucial. As an investor, house hunter, flipper, landlord, or property manager, finding the right mortgage for your investment property can greatly impact your profitability and success in the real estate market. In this subchapter, we will delve into the various mortgage options available to help you make informed decisions and maximize your returns.

From House Hunter to Landlord:
The Complete Handbook for Property Investment in 2024

1. Traditional Mortgage: This is the most common type of mortgage used for investment properties. With a traditional mortgage, you can secure financing from a bank or lending institution by putting down a substantial down payment (typically 20% to 25% of the property's value). This mortgage option offers competitive interest rates and terms, making it a popular choice among investors.

2. Portfolio Lenders: Unlike traditional mortgages, portfolio lenders are not bound by the strict guidelines imposed by government-sponsored enterprises such as Fannie Mae or Freddie Mac. These lenders offer more flexibility in terms of loan qualification criteria, making them ideal for investors with unique circumstances or non-traditional income sources.

3. Hard Money Loans: If you are looking to flip properties or need quick financing, hard money loans can be a viable option. These short-term, high-interest loans are typically provided by private individuals or companies and are secured by the property itself. While hard money loans come with higher interest rates, they offer faster approval and funding, making them suitable for investors who need to act swiftly.

4. FHA 203(k) Loans: If you are a house hunter looking to purchase a fixer-upper, FHA 203(k) loans could be the perfect solution. These government-backed loans allow you to finance both the purchase and renovation costs of the property in a single mortgage. With a low down payment requirement and favorable terms, FHA 203(k) loans are an attractive option for investors looking to maximize their returns through property rehabilitation.

5. Seller Financing: In some cases, sellers may be willing to finance the purchase themselves, eliminating the need for traditional mortgages. With seller financing, the buyer pays the seller directly over time, typically with a down payment and agreed-upon interest rate. This option can be beneficial for investors who have limited access to traditional financing or want to negotiate more favorable terms.

Understanding the mortgage options available for single-family home rental property investment is crucial in maximizing your returns and achieving long-term success. By exploring these various avenues, you can make informed decisions that align with your investment goals and financial circumstances. Remember to consult with mortgage professionals and conduct thorough research to ensure you choose the option that best suits your needs.

Understanding Loan-to-Value Ratios and Down Payment Requirements

From House Hunter to Landlord:
The Complete Handbook for Property Investment in 2024

In the world of real estate investment, understanding the loan-to-value (LTV) ratio and down payment requirements is crucial. Whether you're an investor, house hunter, flipper, landlord, or property manager, knowing these key concepts can make or break your success in the single-family home rental property investment niche.

The loan-to-value ratio is a financial metric used by lenders to assess the risk of a potential loan. It represents the ratio between the loan amount and the appraised value of the property. For example, if you're seeking a loan of $200,000 and the property is appraised at $250,000, the LTV ratio would be 80%. Lenders often have specific LTV requirements, as a higher ratio indicates a riskier investment. Understanding the LTV ratio allows you to evaluate your borrowing capacity and negotiate favorable loan terms.

Down payment requirements are closely tied to the LTV ratio. When purchasing a property, you'll need to make a down payment to secure the loan. The down payment is a percentage of the property's purchase price that you pay upfront. Generally, a larger down payment reduces the LTV ratio and demonstrates your commitment to the investment. For example, if the lender requires a 20% down payment on a $250,000 property, you would need to pay $50,000 upfront.

Why are these concepts important for single-family home rental property investment? Well, they determine your financial commitment and influence your potential returns. A lower LTV ratio and a higher down payment can lead to lower interest rates, reduced monthly mortgage payments, and increased cash flow. On the other hand, a higher LTV ratio and a smaller down payment may result in higher borrowing costs and reduced profitability.

Additionally, understanding the LTV ratio and down payment requirements helps you assess the risk associated with your investment. A lower LTV ratio means you have more equity in the property, providing a buffer against market fluctuations. It also reduces the likelihood of being underwater on your loan, where the outstanding balance exceeds the property's value.

In conclusion, comprehending the loan-to-value ratio and down payment requirements is essential for success in the single-family home rental property investment niche. These concepts allow you to evaluate your borrowing capacity, negotiate favorable loan terms, and assess the risk associated with your investment. By understanding and strategically utilizing these financial metrics, you can maximize your returns and build a profitable rental property portfolio.

Evaluating the Pros and Cons of Fixed-Rate and Adjustable-Rate Mortgages

When it comes to financing your single-family home rental property investment, there are two main options to consider: fixed-rate mortgages and adjustable-rate mortgages (ARMs). Each option has its own set of advantages and disadvantages, and as an investor, house hunter, flipper, landlord, or property manager, it is important to understand the pros and cons of both before making a decision.

Fixed-rate mortgages are the most popular choice for many property investors due to their stability and predictability. With a fixed-rate mortgage, the interest rate remains the same throughout the life of the loan, allowing you to budget your expenses accurately. This consistency provides peace of mind, especially in times of economic uncertainty when interest rates may fluctuate. Additionally, fixed-rate mortgages offer protection against rising interest rates, ensuring that your monthly mortgage payments remain unchanged.

However, the main drawback of fixed-rate mortgages is that they typically come with higher interest rates compared to ARMs. This means you may end up paying more in interest over the life of the loan. Additionally, if interest rates drop significantly after you secure a fixed-rate mortgage, you will not be able to take advantage of these lower rates without refinancing, which can be costly and time-consuming.

On the other hand, adjustable-rate mortgages (ARMs) offer lower initial interest rates, making them an attractive option for many property investors. ARMs typically have a fixed rate for an initial period, such as five or seven years, after which the rate adjusts periodically based on market conditions. If interest rates are expected to decrease or remain stable in the future, an ARM can be a smart choice, as it allows you to take advantage of lower rates over time.

However, the main downside of ARMs is the uncertainty that comes with adjustable rates. As the interest rate adjusts periodically, your monthly mortgage payments can increase significantly, potentially putting a strain on your cash flow. This unpredictability can make budgeting more challenging and may affect your ability to cover other property-related expenses.

In conclusion, the decision between a fixed-rate mortgage and an adjustable-rate mortgage depends on your individual circumstances and investment goals. If you prioritize stability and predictability, a fixed-rate mortgage may be the way to go. However, if you are comfortable with a level of uncertainty and believe that interest rates may decrease in the future, an adjustable-rate mortgage can offer potential cost savings. Regardless of your choice, it is essential to carefully evaluate your financial situation and consult with a mortgage professional to select the option that aligns best with your property investment strategy.

Utilizing Creative Financing Strategies and Working with Private Lenders

When it comes to investing in single-family home rental properties, one of the biggest hurdles for many individuals is securing financing. Traditional lenders often have strict criteria and high-interest rates, making it challenging for investors, house hunters, flippers, landlords, and property managers to acquire the funds they need. However, with the right knowledge and strategies, you can overcome these obstacles and achieve your property investment goals.

This subchapter will delve into the world of creative financing strategies and the benefits of working with private lenders. By understanding these concepts and implementing them effectively, you'll be well on your way to building a successful portfolio of rental properties.

Creative financing strategies are alternative methods to obtain funding that go beyond the traditional bank loan. These strategies include options such as owner financing, lease options, subject-to deals, and hard money loans. Each strategy has its own advantages and considerations, and it's crucial to evaluate which one aligns best with your investment goals and risk tolerance.

Owner financing, for instance, allows you to negotiate directly with the property seller, eliminating the need for a traditional mortgage. This can be a win–win situation, as it provides the seller with a steady income stream while giving you the opportunity to secure a property without jumping through the hoops of conventional financing.

Another creative financing option is working with private lenders. Unlike banks, private lenders are individuals or organizations that provide loans for real estate investments. They often offer more flexible terms, faster approval processes, and customized repayment plans. Building relationships with private lenders is crucial for property investors, as they can provide the necessary capital to fund your acquisitions and renovations.

This subchapter will guide you through the process of identifying and connecting with private lenders, establishing trust, and presenting your investment opportunities in a compelling manner. It will also cover the importance of building a solid reputation and track record to attract private lenders who are eager to invest in your projects.

In conclusion, creative financing strategies and working with private lenders are essential tools for individuals involved in single-family home rental property investment. By expanding your understanding of these techniques and embracing their potential, you can overcome financing challenges, seize lucrative opportunities, and ultimately build a profitable and diverse property portfolio.

Chapter 6: Acquiring and Negotiating Property Purchases

Making Offers and Negotiating Purchase Agreements

When it comes to single-family home rental property investment, one of the most critical stages is making offers and negotiating purchase agreements. This step involves careful planning, market analysis, and effective negotiation skills to secure the best deal possible. In this subchapter, we will delve into the key strategies and tactics that investors, house hunters, flippers, landlords, and property managers can employ to navigate this crucial phase of property investment.

Before diving into making offers, it is imperative to conduct thorough market research. This entails analyzing comparable sales, rental rates, and property appreciation trends in the target area. Armed with this knowledge, investors can determine the fair market value of a property and make informed offers that align with their investment goals.

Once an investor identifies a property of interest, they must craft a compelling offer. This involves carefully considering factors such as the desired purchase price, contingencies, financing terms, and any additional conditions necessary to protect their interests. Crafting a well-structured offer demonstrates professionalism and increases the likelihood of acceptance.

Negotiating purchase agreements requires effective communication and negotiation skills. Understanding the seller's motivations and being able to address their concerns can be instrumental in reaching a mutually beneficial agreement. This subchapter will provide a comprehensive guide to negotiating strategies, including leveraging market conditions, understanding seller psychology, and employing effective communication techniques to secure the best possible outcome.

Furthermore, it is crucial to be aware of common pitfalls and challenges that may arise during the negotiation process. This subchapter will shed light on potential obstacles and offer practical solutions to overcome them. From dealing with counteroffers to managing contingencies, readers will gain valuable insights into navigating the negotiation phase successfully.

Lastly, we will explore the importance of engaging qualified professionals during the negotiation process. Real estate agents, attorneys, and property inspectors play crucial roles in ensuring a smooth transaction. This subchapter will provide guidance on selecting the right professionals and leveraging their expertise to secure favorable purchase agreements.

In conclusion, making offers and negotiating purchase agreements is an integral part of single-family home rental property investment. By arming themselves with market knowledge, employing effective negotiation strategies, and enlisting the right professionals, investors, house hunters, flippers, landlords, and property managers can confidently navigate this critical stage of property investment, ensuring their success in the competitive real estate market.

Understanding Contingencies and Escrow Processes

From House Hunter to Landlord:
The Complete Handbook for Property Investment in 2024

When it comes to investing in single-family home rental properties, it is crucial to have a comprehensive understanding of contingencies and the escrow process. These two aspects play a vital role in ensuring a smooth and successful property investment journey. Whether you are an investor, house hunter, flipper, landlord, or property manager, this subchapter will provide you with the necessary knowledge to navigate contingencies and escrow processes effectively.

Contingencies are conditions that must be met for a real estate transaction to move forward. They protect both the buyer and the seller and allow either party to back out of the deal if the conditions are not met. As an investor or house hunter, it is essential to identify and understand the various contingencies that can be included in a purchase agreement. These may include financing contingencies, inspection contingencies, or even contingencies related to the sale of another property. By comprehending these contingencies, you can ensure that you are protected throughout the buying process, minimizing any potential risks or losses.

Escrow processes, on the other hand, involve a neutral third party handling the funds and documentation related to the real estate transaction. This third party ensures that all conditions of the purchase agreement are met before releasing the funds to the seller. As an investor or flipper, understanding the escrow process is crucial to ensure a smooth closing. This includes knowing the necessary documents, timelines, and potential pitfalls that may arise during the process. By being well-versed in escrow processes, you can avoid delays, legal issues, or financial losses that may occur if mishandled.

In this subchapter, we will delve into the intricacies of contingencies and escrow processes. We will explore the different types of contingencies that may arise in a single-family home rental property investment and how to navigate them effectively. Additionally, we will provide you with a step-by-step breakdown of the escrow process, highlighting the essential documents and considerations along the way.

By the end of this subchapter, you will have a comprehensive understanding of contingencies and escrow processes, empowering you to make informed decisions and ensure a successful property investment journey. Whether you are a first-time investor or an experienced property manager, this knowledge will prove invaluable in your quest for financial success and growth in the single-family home rental property niche.

Conducting Property Appraisals and Title Searches

One of the most critical steps in the property investment process is conducting thorough property appraisals and title searches. These tasks are essential for investors, house hunters, flippers, landlords, and property managers, particularly those focusing on single-family home rental property investment. By understanding the significance of these processes, you can ensure a successful and profitable venture in the real estate market.

When conducting property appraisals, it is crucial to assess the market value of the property accurately. This evaluation will help determine if the property is priced appropriately and if it has the potential to generate positive cash flow. Appraisals involve analyzing various factors, including the property's location, condition, size, amenities, and recent sales of comparable properties in the area. By hiring a professional appraiser or using reliable valuation tools, investors can obtain an unbiased estimate of the property's worth.

Equally important is conducting thorough title searches before finalizing any property purchase. Title searches help identify any legal issues or encumbrances that may affect the property's ownership or marketability. These searches typically involve researching public records, including deeds, liens, mortgages, and easements, to ensure there are no outstanding claims or disputes associated with the property. By uncovering any potential title issues in advance, investors can avoid costly legal battles or unexpected financial burdens in the future.

Investors and property managers must also consider the potential risks and challenges associated with property appraisals and title searches. For instance, if an appraisal comes in lower than expected, it may be necessary to renegotiate the purchase price or reassess the property's investment potential. Similarly, title searches can uncover hidden issues, such as undisclosed liens or property line disputes, which may require legal resolution. Being aware of these risks and having contingency plans in place will allow investors to navigate potential obstacles effectively.

In conclusion, conducting property appraisals and title searches is a vital aspect of single-family home rental property investment. These processes provide investors, house hunters, flippers, landlords, and property managers with valuable insights into a property's value, potential cash flow, and legal status. By allocating sufficient time and resources to these tasks, investors can minimize risks, make informed decisions, and ultimately achieve success in their property investment endeavors.

Closing the Deal and Transferring Ownership

Closing the deal and transferring ownership is a critical phase in the process of property investment, whether you are an investor, house hunter, flipper, landlord, or property manager. In this subchapter, we will delve into the key considerations and steps involved in successfully closing a deal for single-family home rental property investment.

1. Negotiating the Purchase:
Before closing the deal, it is important to negotiate the purchase terms that align with your investment goals. This includes determining the purchase price, financing options, contingencies, and any repairs or improvements required before finalizing the sale. As an investor, it is crucial to conduct thorough due diligence to ensure the property's value matches the asking price.

2. Securing Financing:
Securing financing is a crucial step in closing the deal. As a house hunter or investor, you need to explore various financing options available to you, such as traditional mortgages, private loans, or partnerships. It is essential to compare interest rates, terms, and closing costs to make an informed decision that suits your financial situation.

3. Conducting a Title Search:
Performing a title search is vital to ensure the property's ownership is clear and free from any liens, encumbrances, or legal issues. This step protects your investment and guarantees a smooth transfer of ownership. Engage a professional title search company or attorney to thoroughly examine the property's history and address any potential concerns.

4. Preparing Closing Documents:
Closing documents include the purchase agreement, loan documents, title documents, and any other legal paperwork required to complete the transaction. It is advisable to seek legal counsel to ensure all necessary documents are prepared accurately and in compliance with local laws and regulations.

5. Closing the Deal:
The actual closing involves the transfer of ownership from the seller to the buyer. This typically takes place at a title company, attorney's office, or in some cases, online. During the closing, all parties involved sign the necessary documents, and the buyer pays the agreed-upon amount. Upon completion, the property officially changes hands, and ownership is transferred.

6. Post-Closing Responsibilities:
After closing, there are several post-closing responsibilities that need attention. This includes updating property insurance, transferring utilities, notifying tenants (if applicable), and ensuring all necessary permits and licenses are obtained. As a landlord or property manager, it is crucial to establish a comprehensive plan for managing the property effectively and maximizing your return on investment.

Closing the deal and transferring ownership is a significant milestone in the property investment journey. By understanding and following the steps outlined in this subchapter, you will be well-equipped to navigate the complexities of closing a deal for a single-family home rental property investment. Remember, thorough research, careful negotiation, and attention to detail are key to a successful transaction that sets you on the path to financial success in the real estate market.

Chapter 7: Preparing and Renovating Your Rental Property

Creating a Renovation Budget and Timeline

When it comes to investing in single-family home rental properties, one of the most crucial aspects that can make or break your success is the renovation process. Renovations not only enhance the value and appeal of the property but also ensure that it attracts quality tenants and provides a good return on investment. To achieve this, it is essential to create a renovation budget and timeline that allows you to stay organized and on track throughout the process.

First and foremost, as an investor, house hunter, flipper, landlord, or property manager, it is crucial to have a clear understanding of your financial capabilities and constraints. Take the time to thoroughly analyze your available funds and determine how much you are willing to invest in the renovation project. A prudent approach is to allocate a percentage of the property's purchase price for renovations, ensuring that you don't overspend and leave room for potential unexpected expenses.

Once you have a budget in mind, it is time to create a comprehensive renovation timeline. Start by assessing the property and identifying the areas that require immediate attention. Categorize the renovations into two groups: those that are essential for safety and functionality, and those that are cosmetic and can be done later. This will help you prioritize your tasks and allocate the necessary time and resources accordingly.

Consider consulting with professionals, such as contractors, architects, or interior designers, to get accurate estimates and expert advice on the scope of work involved. Their input will be valuable in determining the duration and cost of each renovation task. Be sure to factor in any necessary permits or inspections that may be required, as overlooking these can lead to costly delays or fines.

Maintaining a well-organized renovation schedule is crucial to staying on track. Break down the timeline into smaller milestones, setting deadlines for each task. This will help you monitor progress and take corrective action if necessary. Additionally, consider creating a contingency plan to account for unexpected delays or cost overruns that may arise during the renovation process.

Throughout the renovation, ensure effective communication and coordination with your contractors and suppliers. Regularly review and update your budget and timeline, making adjustments as needed. By proactively managing the renovation process, you can save time, money, and potential headaches down the road.

In conclusion, creating a renovation budget and timeline is a crucial step for any investor, house hunter, flipper, landlord, or property manager looking to maximize their success in single-family home rental property investments. By thoroughly assessing your financial capabilities, prioritizing renovations, seeking professional advice, and maintaining a well-organized schedule, you can ensure a smooth and efficient renovation process that enhances your property's value and profitability.

Identifying Essential Repairs and Upgrades for Rental Properties

As an investor, house hunter, flipper, landlord, or property manager focused on single-family home rental property investment, it is crucial to understand the importance of identifying and implementing essential repairs and upgrades. This subchapter aims to guide you through the process of evaluating your rental property to maximize its potential and attract quality tenants.

From House Hunter to Landlord:
The Complete Handbook for Property Investment in 2024

First and foremost, conducting a thorough property inspection is vital. Start by assessing the overall condition of the property, including the roof, foundation, plumbing, electrical systems, and HVAC. Look for any signs of damage, leaks, or outdated equipment that may require attention. Identifying these issues early on will help you prioritize repairs and allocate your budget effectively.

Next, consider the functional aspects of the rental property. Ensure that all appliances, fixtures, and utilities are in proper working condition. This includes checking for leaky faucets, malfunctioning appliances, faulty outlets, and poor water pressure. The goal is to provide a safe and comfortable living environment for your tenants, which will enhance tenant satisfaction and reduce turnover.

Additionally, evaluate the aesthetic appeal of the property. Consider repainting the walls, replacing worn-out flooring, and updating outdated fixtures. Curb appeal is equally important, as it significantly influences a potential tenant's first impression. Enhancing the property's exterior with landscaping, fresh paint, and a well-maintained yard can attract higher-quality tenants and potentially increase rental income.

When considering upgrades, focus on features that offer long-term benefits. Energy-efficient upgrades, such as installing LED lighting, programmable thermostats, or energy-saving appliances, can not only attract environmentally-conscious tenants but also save on utility costs, increasing your property's profitability.

Remember to document all repairs and upgrades made to the rental property. This will not only help you keep track of your expenses but also provide valuable information when marketing the property to potential tenants. By highlighting the newly renovated aspects, you can showcase the property's value and attract tenants who are willing to pay a premium for a well-maintained home.

In conclusion, identifying essential repairs and upgrades for your single-family home rental property is crucial to ensure its profitability and attract high-quality tenants. Conduct thorough inspections, address functional issues, enhance the property's aesthetic appeal, and consider energy-efficient upgrades. By investing in these essential repairs and upgrades, you will create a desirable living space, increase tenant satisfaction, and maximize your return on investment.

Working with Contractors, Architects, and Designers

When it comes to investing in single-family home rental properties, one of the most crucial aspects of success lies in working effectively with contractors, architects, and designers. These professionals play a vital role in transforming your property into a desirable and profitable rental. In this subchapter, we will explore the key considerations and strategies for collaborating with these experts.

First and foremost, it is essential to establish a clear vision for your property investment project. Before engaging with contractors, architects, or designers, take the time to outline your goals, budget, and timeline. This will serve as a foundation for effective communication and collaboration throughout the project.

To find the right professionals for your project, network within your local real estate community and seek recommendations from fellow investors, house hunters, flippers, landlords, and property managers. Look for contractors, architects, and designers with experience in single-family home rental property investment. They should have a strong portfolio that demonstrates their ability to deliver quality work within budget and on schedule.

When working with contractors, ensure that you have a detailed contract in place. This should include project scope, timeline, budget, payment terms, and any warranties or guarantees. Regularly communicate with your contractor, providing feedback and addressing any concerns promptly. This will help maintain a healthy working relationship and ensure that the project stays on track.

Architects and designers are instrumental in enhancing the aesthetic appeal and functionality of your rental property. Collaborate closely with them to create a cohesive design that aligns with your target market and rental goals. Consider factors such as layout, color scheme, fixtures, and finishes to attract tenants and maximize rental income.

Throughout the process, be attentive to your budget and timeline. Regularly review the progress, expenses, and potential delays to ensure that you are staying within your financial constraints and projected completion date.

Working with contractors, architects, and designers can be a valuable investment in your single-family home rental property. Their expertise can significantly impact the desirability and profitability of your rental. By establishing clear goals, finding the right professionals, and maintaining strong communication throughout the project, you can ensure a successful collaboration that yields impressive results.

Remember, a well-designed and meticulously executed rental property will not only attract high-quality tenants but also command higher rental rates, ultimately maximizing your return on investment.

Maximizing Property Value and Appeal through Renovations

Renovating a single-family home rental property can be a lucrative investment strategy. By making strategic improvements, you can increase its value and appeal to potential tenants, ultimately maximizing your return on investment. In this subchapter, we will discuss various renovation ideas and tips to help you make the most out of your property investment.

1. Assess the property: Before diving into renovations, start by evaluating the property's condition. Identify any areas that require immediate attention, such as plumbing or electrical issues. This initial assessment will help you prioritize renovations and allocate your budget efficiently.

2. Enhance curb appeal: First impressions matter. Boost the property's exterior appearance by investing in landscaping, fresh paint, a new front door, and updated lighting fixtures. These simple changes can significantly improve the property's overall appeal and draw in potential tenants.

3. Kitchen and bathroom upgrades: Renovating kitchens and bathrooms can have a substantial impact on a property's value. Consider updating countertops, cabinets, appliances, and fixtures to give these spaces a modern and attractive look. Pay attention to functionality and durability when selecting materials, as they should withstand regular wear and tear.

4. Flooring and paint: Replace outdated flooring with durable and visually appealing options such as hardwood or laminate. Additionally, a fresh coat of paint throughout the property can instantly revitalize its look and make it more inviting to prospective tenants.

5. Energy-efficient upgrades: Go green to attract environmentally-conscious tenants and reduce utility costs. Consider installing energy-efficient appliances, LED lighting, programmable thermostats, and low-flow plumbing fixtures. These upgrades not only enhance the property's value but also appeal to tenants looking to reduce their carbon footprint.

6. Maximizing space: Open floor plans are highly sought after by modern tenants. If possible, knock down walls to create an open and spacious layout. Additionally, consider utilizing underutilized spaces, such as basements and attics, to add extra living areas or storage space.

7. Smart home technology: Incorporating smart home devices, such as security systems, thermostats, and smart locks, can attract tech-savvy tenants and increase the property's desirability.

Remember to research local market trends and preferences when planning renovations. Understanding your target audience is crucial to ensure that your investment aligns with their needs and desires. By maximizing property value and appeal through strategic renovations, you can attract quality tenants and enjoy a profitable single-family home rental property investment.

Chapter 8: Marketing and Tenant Screening

Developing Effective Marketing Strategies for Rental Properties

Introduction:
Marketing plays a crucial role in the success of any rental property investment. In this subchapter, we will explore the various strategies and techniques that can help investors, house hunters, flippers, landlords, and property managers develop effective marketing strategies for single-family home rental properties. By implementing these strategies, you can attract high-quality tenants, maximize occupancy rates, and increase your rental income.

From House Hunter to Landlord:
The Complete Handbook for Property Investment in 2024

Understanding the Target Audience:
Before diving into marketing tactics, it is essential to understand your target audience. Consider the demographics, lifestyle preferences, and needs of potential tenants in your area. This knowledge will help you tailor your marketing efforts to attract the right tenants for your single-family home rental property.

Creating an Online Presence:
In today's digital age, having a strong online presence is crucial for marketing rental properties. Develop a professional website that showcases your property's features, amenities, and location. Utilize high-quality photographs and create compelling descriptions to captivate potential tenants. Additionally, leverage social media platforms to reach a wider audience and engage with potential tenants.

Utilizing Online Listings and Directories:
Listing your rental property on popular real estate websites and online directories is another effective marketing strategy. These platforms attract a large number of house hunters and tenants actively searching for rental properties. Ensure your listings are accurate, detailed, and regularly updated to maintain visibility and attract potential tenants.

From House Hunter to Landlord:
The Complete Handbook for Property Investment in 2024

Harnessing the Power of Word-of-Mouth:
Word-of-mouth marketing can be a powerful tool in attracting tenants. Encourage your current tenants to refer your property to their friends, family, and colleagues. Consider offering incentives, such as discounted rent or referral bonuses, to motivate them further. Additionally, maintain positive relationships with your tenants to foster a good reputation within the community.

Partnering with Local Businesses:
Collaborating with local businesses can help you reach potential tenants in your area. Establish relationships with nearby employers, universities, and relocation agencies. Offer them incentives, such as exclusive discounts or referral programs, to recommend your rental property to their employees or students.

Monitoring and Analyzing Marketing Efforts:
To ensure the effectiveness of your marketing strategies, it is essential to monitor and analyze your efforts regularly. Track the performance of your online listings, website analytics, and lead conversion rates. Use this data to identify areas for improvement and refine your marketing strategies accordingly.

Conclusion:
Developing effective marketing strategies for single-family home rental properties is essential for attracting high-quality tenants and maximizing your rental income. By understanding your target audience, creating an online presence, utilizing online listings, harnessing word-of-mouth marketing, partnering with local businesses, and monitoring your marketing efforts, you can significantly enhance your property's visibility and attract the right tenants. Implement these strategies to ensure a successful and profitable rental property investment journey.

Attracting High-Quality Tenants through Advertising and Showings

As an investor, house hunter, flipper, landlord, or property manager specializing in single-family home rental property investments, one of your primary goals is to attract high-quality tenants. To achieve this, effective advertising and showings play a pivotal role in showcasing the value of your property and attracting the right individuals or families.

From House Hunter to Landlord:
The Complete Handbook for Property Investment in 2024

Advertising is your first opportunity to make a lasting impression. Start by crafting compelling property listings that highlight the unique features and benefits of your rental home. Begin with an attention-grabbing headline that emphasizes the property's key selling points, such as "Charming 3-Bedroom Home with Modern Upgrades in Desirable Neighborhood." Provide a detailed but concise description that covers the home's amenities, nearby conveniences, and any recent renovations or upgrades. Use professional-quality photos that showcase the property's best angles and ensure they are well-lit and clutter-free.

Now that your advertisement is enticing, it's time to schedule showings to attract potential tenants. Make it easy for interested individuals to view the property by offering convenient times, including evenings and weekends. Consider hosting open houses to accommodate multiple prospective tenants at once. Prepare the property beforehand by ensuring it is clean, well-maintained, and staged attractively. A well-presented home gives tenants confidence in your professionalism and the quality of your property.

During showings, adopt a friendly and approachable demeanor to build rapport with potential tenants. Answer their questions promptly and honestly, highlighting the unique features and benefits of the property. Be prepared to provide information on nearby schools, shopping centers, parks, and transportation options – these details can greatly influence a tenant's decision-making process.

To attract high-quality tenants, you must also conduct thorough tenant screenings. Request completed rental applications from interested parties and verify their employment, income, and rental history. Perform background checks and credit assessments to ensure financial stability and reliability. By implementing rigorous screening procedures, you can mitigate the risk of potential issues in the future.

Remember, attracting high-quality tenants is not only about finding individuals or families who can pay the rent consistently, but also those who will treat your property with respect and care. By investing time and effort into advertising and showings, you are setting the stage for a successful landlord-tenant relationship that benefits both parties in the long run.

Conducting Thorough Tenant Screening and Background Checks

As an investor, house hunter, flipper, landlord, or property manager in the niche of single-family home rental property investment, one crucial aspect of your success lies in conducting thorough tenant screening and background checks. This subchapter will guide you through the process, ensuring that you select reliable and responsible tenants who will help protect your investment and provide a steady stream of rental income.

When it comes to tenant screening, the first step is to establish clear criteria for potential tenants. This includes factors such as income verification, credit history, rental history, and criminal background checks. By setting specific requirements, you can quickly filter out applicants who don't meet your standards, saving time and effort in the long run.

Income verification is essential to ensure that tenants have a stable financial standing to meet their rental obligations. Requesting pay stubs or employment verification can help confirm their income and employment stability. Similarly, checking their credit history will provide insights into their financial responsibility, including any outstanding debts or previous evictions.

Rental history can also provide valuable information about a tenant's behavior and reliability. Contacting previous landlords will allow you to gain insights into their rental payment history, any complaints or damages caused, and their overall conduct as tenants. This step is crucial in identifying potential red flags and avoiding problematic tenants.

Furthermore, conducting criminal background checks is crucial to ensure the safety and well-being of both your property and other tenants. This step helps identify any history of criminal activities or violent behavior that may pose a risk to the community. Remember to comply with fair housing laws and treat all applicants equally during this process.

To streamline the screening process, consider utilizing online tenant screening services or hiring professional screening agencies. These services can provide comprehensive reports on an applicant's credit, rental, and criminal history, saving you time and effort.

By conducting thorough tenant screening and background checks, you can minimize the risk of property damage, late payments, and eviction costs. Remember, investing time and effort into this process upfront will pay off in the long run by securing reliable tenants who will treat your property with care and uphold their rental obligations.

Crafting Lease Agreements and Setting Rental Terms

When it comes to single-family home rental property investment, crafting lease agreements and setting rental terms is an essential step for investors, house hunters, flippers, landlords, and property managers alike. A well-structured lease agreement not only protects the rights of both parties involved but also ensures a smooth and profitable rental experience.

One of the first considerations when crafting a lease agreement is to clearly outline the terms and conditions of the rental property. This includes specifying the rental period, monthly rent amount, and any additional fees or charges the tenant may be responsible for. It is crucial to be thorough and explicit in detailing these terms to avoid any potential conflicts or misunderstandings in the future.

In addition to the basic terms, it is also important to establish guidelines for property maintenance and repairs. Clearly outline the responsibilities of both the tenant and the landlord in terms of maintenance and repairs, and include procedures for reporting and addressing issues that may arise during the tenancy. This will help ensure that the property is well-maintained and any necessary repairs are addressed promptly.

Another key aspect of lease agreements is setting rules and regulations for the property. This may include guidelines on noise levels, pet policies, and restrictions on alterations or modifications to the property. Clearly communicating these rules to tenants upfront can help avoid potential conflicts and ensure a harmonious living environment for all parties involved.

Furthermore, it is essential to address the issue of security deposits in the lease agreement. Specify the amount of the deposit, the conditions under which it will be forfeited, and the timeline for its return. Clearly outlining these terms will help protect the landlord's interests while providing transparency to the tenant.

Finally, it is important to include provisions for lease termination and renewal in the agreement. Clearly state the notice period required for termination or renewal, as well as any penalties or fees that may apply. This will provide both parties with a clear understanding of their rights and obligations in relation to the lease term.

Crafting lease agreements and setting rental terms is a crucial step in single-family home rental property investment. By providing clarity and transparency to both parties, a well-crafted lease agreement can help ensure a successful and profitable rental experience. Whether you are an investor, house hunter, flipper, landlord, or property manager, understanding the importance of lease agreements and rental terms is essential in building a strong foundation for your property investment journey.

Chapter 9: Managing Rental Properties and Tenant Relations

Establishing Effective Property Management Systems and Processes

When it comes to single-family home rental property investment, one of the key factors in ensuring your success is establishing effective property management systems and processes. Whether you're an investor, house hunter, flipper, landlord, or property manager, having a solid foundation in property management is crucial for maximizing your returns and minimizing your headaches.

First and foremost, it's important to understand that property management is not a passive endeavor. It requires active involvement and a systematic approach to ensure that your properties are well-maintained, tenants are satisfied, and your investment is protected. This subchapter will guide you through the essential steps in setting up and implementing effective property management systems and processes.

To begin, it's essential to have a clear understanding of your goals and objectives as a property investor. Are you looking for long-term stability and cash flow, or are you more interested in short-term gains through flipping properties? This will determine the type of properties you acquire and the management systems you put in place.

Next, you need to establish a thorough screening process for potential tenants. This includes conducting background and credit checks, verifying employment and income, and checking references. By ensuring that you have reliable and responsible tenants, you can avoid many potential issues and headaches down the line.

Additionally, having a comprehensive lease agreement is vital. This document should clearly outline the responsibilities of both the landlord and the tenant, including rent payment terms, maintenance and repair obligations, and any rules or regulations specific to the property. By having a well-defined lease agreement, you can protect both your investment and your relationship with your tenants.

Maintenance and repairs are another critical aspect of property management. Establishing a reliable network of contractors and service providers is essential to ensure that any issues are promptly addressed and resolved. Regular inspections and preventative maintenance can also help you identify and address any potential problems before they become more significant and costly.

Lastly, effective communication is key to successful property management. Establishing clear lines of communication with your tenants, property manager (if applicable), and any other stakeholders involved will help address any concerns or issues in a timely and efficient manner.

In summary, effective property management systems and processes are essential for single-family home rental property investment. By following the steps outlined in this subchapter, you can establish a solid foundation for managing your properties, ensuring tenant satisfaction, and protecting your investment. Remember, property management is an ongoing endeavor, and continuous improvement and adaptation to changing circumstances are necessary for long-term success.

Handling Maintenance and Repairs in a Timely Manner

As an investor, house hunter, flipper, landlord, or property manager, one of the most crucial aspects of managing a single-family home rental property is ensuring that maintenance and repairs are handled promptly and efficiently. Neglecting or delaying these tasks can lead to tenant dissatisfaction, increased expenses, and potential legal issues. In this subchapter, we will explore the key principles and strategies for effectively handling maintenance and repairs on your property investment.

First and foremost, it is essential to establish a proactive approach to maintenance. Regular inspections and preventative measures can help identify potential issues before they become major problems. By conducting routine checks, you can catch minor repairs early on, saving you both time and money in the long run. Encourage open communication with your tenants, as they often notice maintenance issues before you do. Implement a system for tenants to report problems promptly, ensuring that you address their concerns in a timely manner.

To streamline the maintenance process, it is beneficial to build a network of reliable contractors and service providers. Establishing relationships with trustworthy plumbers, electricians, HVAC technicians, and handymen can expedite repairs and ensure quality workmanship. Obtain multiple quotes for larger repairs to ensure fair pricing and avoid unnecessary expenses. Remember, investing in high-quality repairs upfront can save you from frequent and costly repairs in the future.

Maintaining organized records is crucial for efficient property management. Keep detailed documentation of all maintenance and repair requests, expenses, and contractor invoices. This documentation will not only help you track expenses and deductible repairs but will also serve as evidence in case of any legal disputes with tenants.

When it comes to handling repairs, prioritize urgent issues that affect the habitability and safety of the property. A leaking roof, faulty electrical wiring, or a broken HVAC system are examples of repairs that should be addressed immediately. Regularly communicate with your tenants to inform them about the status of repairs and provide realistic timelines for completion.

Lastly, consider implementing a preventative maintenance schedule. Regularly servicing HVAC systems, inspecting the plumbing, and performing seasonal maintenance tasks can help prevent major breakdowns and extend the lifespan of your property's components.

In conclusion, handling maintenance and repairs in a timely manner is crucial for successful single-family home rental property investment. By adopting a proactive approach, building a network of reliable contractors, maintaining organized records, prioritizing urgent repairs, and implementing preventative maintenance, you can ensure the longevity and profitability of your investment. Remember, a well-maintained property leads to satisfied tenants, reduced expenses, and ultimately, a successful property investment venture.

Dealing with Difficult Tenants and Conflict Resolution

As an investor, house hunter, flipper, landlord, or property manager in the niche of single-family home rental property investment, one of the challenges you may encounter is dealing with difficult tenants and conflict resolution. This subchapter aims to equip you with strategies and insights to handle such situations effectively, ensuring a harmonious landlord-tenant relationship.

When it comes to managing difficult tenants, prevention is better than cure. A thorough tenant screening process is your first line of defense. By conducting background checks, verifying income, and contacting references, you can identify potential red flags early on. This step minimizes the likelihood of future conflicts and helps you select tenants who are more likely to respect your property and rental terms.

However, even with the most rigorous screening process, conflicts may still arise. It's crucial to approach these situations with a calm and professional mindset. Communication is key. Actively listen to your tenant's concerns and address them promptly. By acknowledging their issues, you demonstrate your commitment to resolving conflicts and maintaining a positive landlord-tenant relationship.

In some cases, conflicts may escalate, requiring more formal intervention. Familiarize yourself with local landlord-tenant laws, as they provide guidance on dispute resolution. Mediation or arbitration can often be effective alternatives to costly and time-consuming legal proceedings. These methods allow both parties to express their grievances openly and work towards a mutually beneficial resolution.

Another effective strategy for dealing with difficult tenants is to document everything. Maintain clear and comprehensive records of all interactions, including conversations, requests, and repairs. This documentation will serve as evidence in case of future disputes, ensuring transparency and protecting your interests.

In certain situations, eviction may be necessary as a last resort. However, it's essential to follow legal procedures and consult with an attorney to ensure compliance with local laws. Eviction should always be a carefully considered decision, taken only when all other options have been exhausted.

Ultimately, successful conflict resolution with difficult tenants requires a combination of proactive measures, effective communication, and adherence to legal guidelines. By implementing these strategies, you can minimize conflicts, maintain a positive rental experience for both parties, and protect your investment in single-family home rental properties.

Remember, being a landlord is not just about property management; it's also about maintaining healthy relationships with tenants. With the right mindset and tools at your disposal, you can navigate through difficult situations and create a conducive environment for long-term success in property investment.

Understanding Landlord–Tenant Laws and Legal Obligations

As an investor, house hunter, flipper, landlord, or property manager delving into the world of single-family home rental property investment, it is essential to have a solid understanding of landlord–tenant laws and legal obligations. These laws serve as the foundation for a successful and legally compliant rental business, ensuring the protection of both landlords and tenants.

First and foremost, familiarize yourself with the local and state laws governing landlord–tenant relationships. Each jurisdiction has its own set of rules and regulations that dictate landlord responsibilities, tenant rights, and the eviction process, among other crucial aspects. Ignorance of these laws can lead to costly legal battles and tarnish your reputation as a responsible landlord.

One of the most crucial legal obligations is providing habitable living conditions. Landlords must ensure that their rental properties meet certain safety and health standards. This includes proper maintenance, regular inspections, and promptly addressing repairs. Failure to meet these obligations can result in fines, penalties, and even lawsuits from tenants.

Understanding fair housing laws is equally vital. Discrimination based on race, color, religion, sex, national origin, disability, or familial status is strictly prohibited. Familiarize yourself with the federal Fair Housing Act and any additional state or local laws to prevent any unintentional violations. Implementing fair and consistent tenant screening practices will help you avoid potential legal issues.

Additionally, comprehending the eviction process is essential. While eviction should be the last resort, it is sometimes necessary when tenants fail to pay rent, violate lease terms, or cause significant damage to the property. Familiarize yourself with the specific procedures and timelines mandated by your jurisdiction to ensure a smooth and lawful eviction process.

Finally, consider consulting with a qualified real estate attorney to ensure compliance with all relevant laws and regulations. They can provide guidance on lease agreements, tenant disputes, and any legal questions that arise throughout your rental property investment journey.

Remember, understanding landlord-tenant laws and legal obligations is not only a legal requirement but also a means to protect your investment and maintain positive relationships with your tenants. By staying informed and proactive, you can navigate the rental property market successfully and ethically.

Chapter 10: Maximizing Profitability and Long-Term Success

Implementing Strategies for Rent Increases and Lease Renewals

As a property investor or landlord in the single-family home rental market, it is crucial to implement effective strategies for rent increases and lease renewals. This subchapter will provide you with essential insights into these topics, ensuring you maximize your profits and maintain a stable portfolio.

When it comes to rent increases, timing is key. It is recommended to review and adjust rental rates annually to keep up with market trends and inflation. However, it is essential to strike a balance between maximizing your rental income and retaining good tenants. Conducting thorough market research and comparing your property's rental value with similar homes in the area will help you determine a competitive yet reasonable rent increase.

Communication plays a vital role in rent increases and lease renewals. It is crucial to inform your tenants in advance about any upcoming changes to their rental rates. This can be done through written notices or face-to-face meetings, emphasizing the reasons behind the increase, such as rising property taxes or maintenance costs. Maintaining transparency and open lines of communication will foster trust and reduce the likelihood of tenant turnover.

Another strategy to consider is offering incentives for lease renewals. Providing tenants with incentives, such as reduced rent for the first month or minor property upgrades, encourages them to stay longer, minimizing vacancies and turnover costs. Moreover, offering longer lease terms, such as two or three years, can provide stability for both parties and reduce the frequency of rent negotiations.

To streamline the rent increase and lease renewal process, consider utilizing property management software. These tools can automate rent increase notifications, track lease expiration dates, and generate reports on rental income trends. By leveraging technology, you can save time and ensure efficient management of your rental properties.

Lastly, maintaining the quality and appeal of your rental properties is crucial for successful lease renewals. Regular maintenance, prompt response to repair requests, and periodic upgrades will enhance tenant satisfaction and make them more likely to renew their lease. Additionally, consider conducting inspections before lease renewals to identify any necessary repairs or improvements.

In conclusion, implementing effective strategies for rent increases and lease renewals is vital for single-family home rental property investors and landlords. By conducting market research, communicating transparently with tenants, offering incentives, leveraging technology, and prioritizing property maintenance, you can maximize your rental income, retain good tenants, and ensure a successful and profitable investment portfolio.

Minimizing Vacancy Rates and Maximizing Rental Income

When it comes to single-family home rental property investment, one of the key factors that can make or break your success is the ability to minimize vacancy rates and maximize rental income. As an investor, house hunter, flipper, landlord, or property manager, understanding the strategies and techniques to achieve this goal is crucial.

First and foremost, it is essential to attract high-quality tenants who will not only pay their rent on time but also take care of the property. To achieve this, it is crucial to conduct thorough tenant screenings, including background and credit checks, employment verification, and reference checks. By selecting reliable tenants, you can significantly reduce the risk of late payments or property damage, leading to fewer vacancies and higher rental income.

Additionally, maintaining your property in excellent condition is of utmost importance. Regular inspections, prompt repairs, and proactive maintenance not only keep your tenants satisfied but also help you avoid costly repairs down the line. By addressing any issues promptly, you can minimize the chances of tenants leaving due to unresolved problems and maintain a steady stream of rental income.

To maximize rental income, it is essential to stay updated with market trends and adjust your rental rates accordingly. Conducting regular market research and comparing your property's features, location, and amenities to similar rentals in the area will allow you to set competitive rental rates. Offering incentives such as discounted rent for longer leases or pet-friendly policies can also attract tenants and increase your rental income.

Effective communication is another vital aspect of minimizing vacancy rates and maximizing rental income. Maintaining open lines of communication with your tenants ensures that any concerns or maintenance requests are addressed promptly, leading to higher tenant satisfaction and longer tenancy periods. Regularly checking in with your tenants and conducting surveys or feedback sessions can also provide valuable insights for improving your property and services.

Lastly, considering long-term lease agreements with renewal options can provide stability and reduce turnover rates. Offering lease extensions or incentives to reliable tenants who have a good track record can help build a strong tenant-landlord relationship and minimize the chances of vacancy.

In conclusion, minimizing vacancy rates and maximizing rental income is a critical aspect of single-family home rental property investment. By implementing thorough tenant screenings, maintaining the property, staying updated with market trends, establishing effective communication with tenants, and considering long-term lease agreements, you can achieve success in this niche. Remember, investing in your property and cultivating a positive tenant experience will ultimately lead to higher rental income and long-term profitability.

Scaling Your Property Investment Portfolio

In the exciting world of real estate investing, it is essential to have a well-planned strategy for scaling your property investment portfolio. As an investor, house hunter, flipper, landlord, or property manager in the niche of single-family home rental property investment, this subchapter aims to provide you with valuable insights and practical tips to help you achieve growth and success.

1. Establish a Clear Vision: Before embarking on any scaling efforts, it is crucial to define your long-term vision for your property investment portfolio. Consider your financial goals, risk tolerance, and desired timeline for growth. This vision will serve as your compass and guide you in making informed decisions along your investment journey.

2. Build a Strong Foundation: To effectively scale your property investment portfolio, it is essential to establish a solid foundation. This includes conducting thorough market research, understanding local regulations, and building a reliable team of professionals such as real estate agents, property managers, and contractors. By setting up a strong foundation, you can minimize risks and maximize your chances of success.

3. Leverage Financing Options: Scaling your property investment portfolio often requires access to additional capital. Explore various financing options such as traditional mortgages, private lenders, or partnerships to fund your acquisitions. It is crucial to carefully analyze the terms and conditions of each option to ensure they align with your goals and financial capabilities.

4. Diversify Your Portfolio: As you scale your property investment portfolio, consider diversifying your holdings. Investing in different locations, property types, or even exploring commercial real estate can help spread risk and enhance your overall returns. However, ensure you thoroughly research and analyze each potential investment to make informed decisions.

5. Implement Efficient Systems: Scaling a property investment portfolio requires effective systems and processes to manage your properties efficiently. Utilize property management software, automate rent collection, and establish clear communication channels with tenants. By implementing efficient systems, you can streamline operations and free up time for further growth.

6. Continuously Educate Yourself: The real estate market is constantly evolving, and as a property investor, it is crucial to stay updated with the latest trends, regulations, and investment strategies. Attend seminars, read books, and network with industry professionals to expand your knowledge and make informed decisions.

In conclusion, scaling your property investment portfolio in the niche of single-family home rental properties requires careful planning, strategic decision-making, and continuous education. By establishing a clear vision, building a strong foundation, leveraging financing options, diversifying your holdings, implementing efficient systems, and staying informed, you can set yourself up for long-term success and achieve your financial goals.

Planning for Property Appreciation and Exit Strategies

When it comes to property investment, maximizing profits is the ultimate goal. As an investor, house hunter, flipper, landlord, or property manager in the niche of single-family home rental property investment, it is crucial to plan for property appreciation and have a well-thought-out exit strategy. This subchapter will guide you through the essential steps to ensure your investment yields the best possible returns.

First and foremost, understanding property appreciation is key. Property values can increase over time due to various factors such as location, infrastructure development, economic growth, and market trends. Before making any investment, thorough research and analysis of the local real estate market are essential. This will help you identify properties with the potential for long-term appreciation, ensuring your investment grows over time.

To plan for property appreciation, it is crucial to consider several factors. Location is paramount. Properties situated in desirable neighborhoods with good schools, amenities, and transportation links tend to appreciate more rapidly. Additionally, keeping an eye on local development plans, upcoming infrastructure projects, and economic trends can provide valuable insights into potential appreciation.

While property appreciation plays a significant role in maximizing profits, having a solid exit strategy is equally important. An exit strategy refers to a predetermined plan of action to sell or dispose of the property when the time is right. This strategy should align with your investment goals and the market conditions.

One common exit strategy is the buy–and–hold approach, where you acquire properties for long–term rental income. This strategy allows you to benefit from both cash flow and appreciation. On the other hand, some investors prefer the fix–and–flip strategy, which involves purchasing undervalued properties, renovating them, and selling them quickly for a profit. This strategy requires a keen eye for finding distressed properties and understanding the local market demands.

Another popular exit strategy is refinancing. As property values appreciate, you can refinance the property to access the equity and reinvest it into additional properties or other investment opportunities, allowing you to accelerate your portfolio growth.

Regardless of the exit strategy you choose, it is crucial to regularly evaluate your investments and adjust accordingly. Monitoring market trends, rental demand, and property performance will help you make informed decisions and maximize your return on investment.

In conclusion, planning for property appreciation and exit strategies is essential for successful single-family home rental property investment. By understanding the factors influencing property appreciation and having a well-defined exit strategy, you can make informed investment decisions and maximize profits. Remember, research, analysis, and regular evaluation are the keys to thriving in the real estate market.

Chapter 11: The Future of Property Investment

Emerging Trends and Technologies in Real Estate Investing

In the ever-evolving world of real estate investing, staying ahead of the game is crucial. As an investor, house hunter, flipper, landlord, or property manager focused on the niche of single-family home rental property investment, it is essential to keep up with the emerging trends and technologies that can enhance your success in the industry.

From House Hunter to Landlord:
The Complete Handbook for Property Investment in 2024

1. Smart Home Technology: The integration of smart home devices has become a game-changer in the rental market. From smart locks to thermostats and security systems, these technologies not only improve the rental experience for tenants but also provide landlords with enhanced security and energy efficiency. Investing in these technologies can attract tech-savvy tenants and potentially increase rental income.

2. Virtual Reality (VR) and 3D Tours: With the advancements in VR and 3D technology, potential renters can now virtually tour properties from the comfort of their own homes. This not only saves time for both the house hunter and the landlord but also reduces the number of physical showings. Integrating VR and 3D tours into your property marketing strategy can attract a broader audience and increase the chances of finding the perfect tenant.

3. Real Estate Crowdfunding: Real estate crowdfunding platforms have gained popularity in recent years, offering opportunities for investors to pool their resources and invest in properties that were previously inaccessible. These platforms allow investors to diversify their portfolios, access higher-yield properties, and minimize the risks associated with investing in individual properties.

4. Data Analytics and Artificial Intelligence (AI): Leveraging data analytics and AI can provide valuable insights into market trends, property valuation, and tenant preferences. By analyzing large amounts of data, investors and property managers can make informed decisions, identify investment opportunities, and optimize rental strategies.

5. Sustainable and Green Building Practices: As environmental consciousness grows, investing in properties with sustainable and green building practices has become a significant trend. Energy-efficient homes not only attract environmentally conscious tenants but also offer cost savings through reduced utility bills. Integrating sustainable features, such as solar panels or smart thermostats, can add value to your rental property.

6. Short-Term Rentals and Vacation Homes: The rise of platforms like Airbnb has opened up new avenues for real estate investment. Renting out properties for short-term stays or vacation rentals can provide higher rental yields, especially in popular tourist destinations. However, it is crucial to understand the regulations and market demand in your area before venturing into this niche.

To thrive in the world of single-family home rental property investment, it is essential to embrace these emerging trends and technologies. By staying informed and adapting to the changing landscape, investors, house hunters, flippers, landlords, and property managers can maximize their profits, attract quality tenants, and ultimately achieve long-term success in this dynamic industry.

Exploring Alternative Property Investment Opportunities

In the world of real estate investment, the single-family home rental property has long been the go-to choice for investors, house hunters, flippers, landlords, and property managers. However, as the market evolves and new opportunities arise, it is essential to stay ahead of the game by exploring alternative investment options. This subchapter aims to introduce you to some exciting alternatives that can diversify your portfolio and maximize your returns.

1. Multi-family Properties: Instead of focusing solely on single-family homes, consider investing in multi-family properties such as duplexes, triplexes, or apartment complexes. These properties offer multiple rental units under one roof, enabling you to generate higher rental income and spread your risk across multiple tenants.

2. Vacation Rentals: With the rise of platforms like Airbnb and VRBO, vacation rentals have become an attractive investment option. By purchasing properties in high-demand tourist destinations, you can enjoy the benefits of short-term rentals. However, be aware of local regulations and ensure the property's location and amenities align with the preferences of vacationers.

3. Commercial Real Estate: While residential properties are a popular choice, commercial real estate can offer higher returns and long-term stability. Investing in office buildings, shopping centers, or industrial warehouses can provide steady rental income and potential for capital appreciation.

4. Real Estate Investment Trusts (REITs): If you prefer a hands-off approach to property investment, consider investing in REITs. These investment vehicles allow you to own shares in a professionally managed real estate portfolio, providing diversification and liquidity without the responsibilities of property ownership.

5. Real Estate Crowdfunding: Crowdfunding platforms have revolutionized the way individuals invest in real estate. Through these platforms, you can pool your funds with other investors to purchase properties, ranging from residential to commercial. This option allows you to access real estate opportunities with lower capital requirements and reduced risk.

6. Land Investment: Investing in land can be a smart long-term strategy. As population growth continues, the demand for land for development or agriculture is expected to rise. By purchasing land in areas with growth potential, you can benefit from appreciation and potentially sell it to developers or farmers at a higher price.

As an investor, house hunter, flipper, landlord, or property manager, exploring alternative property investment opportunities can provide you with new avenues for financial growth. By diversifying your portfolio and staying open to new trends, you can adapt to changes in the market and maximize your returns.

Adapting to Changing Market Conditions and Economic Factors

In the ever-evolving world of real estate, it is essential for investors, house hunters, flippers, landlords, and property managers to stay abreast of changing market conditions and economic factors. The ability to adapt to these fluctuations is crucial to achieving success in the niche of single-family home rental property investment. This subchapter aims to provide valuable insights and strategies to navigate through these challenges and optimize your property investment endeavors.

Market conditions play a significant role in determining the profitability of your rental property. Understanding supply and demand dynamics, interest rates, and local economic indicators can help you make informed decisions. By conducting thorough market research, you can identify emerging trends, such as the desirability of certain neighborhoods or shifts in rental demand. Armed with this knowledge, you can make smarter buying decisions and capitalize on opportunities before they become mainstream.

Economic factors, including inflation, unemployment rates, and consumer confidence, can greatly impact the rental market. As an investor, it is crucial to monitor these indicators and adjust your investment strategy accordingly. For instance, during periods of economic downturn, you may need to focus on affordable rental properties, while in times of economic growth, you might consider higher-end rentals.

Flexibility is key when adapting to changing market conditions. This involves being open to new ideas, considering alternative investment strategies, and staying ahead of the curve. For example, if the market is saturated with single-family homes for rent, you might explore the potential of multi-family properties or short-term rentals to diversify your portfolio.

Maintaining a proactive approach to property management is also essential. Regularly reviewing rental rates, keeping up with property maintenance, and staying attuned to tenant needs can help you retain quality tenants and maximize your rental income. Additionally, in a dynamic market, it may be necessary to adjust lease terms to stay competitive and attract long-term renters.

Finally, networking with industry professionals, attending real estate seminars, and joining local investor groups can provide valuable insights into market conditions and economic factors affecting the rental property niche. By connecting with like-minded individuals and learning from their experiences, you can enhance your knowledge and make more informed decisions.

In conclusion, adapting to changing market conditions and economic factors is vital for success in the single-family home rental property investment niche. By staying informed, being flexible, and proactively managing your properties, you can maximize your returns and achieve long-term success in the ever-evolving world of real estate investment.

Continuing Education and Networking for Ongoing Success

From House Hunter to Landlord:
The Complete Handbook for Property Investment in 2024

In the fast-paced world of single-family home rental property investment, staying ahead of the game is crucial for long-term success. As an investor, house hunter, flipper, landlord, or property manager, it is essential to recognize the value of continuing education and networking. These two elements will not only enhance your knowledge and skills but also open doors to lucrative opportunities and connections within the industry.

Continuing education is paramount in an ever-evolving real estate market. By actively seeking out educational resources such as books, seminars, webinars, and workshops, you can stay up-to-date with the latest trends, strategies, and legal requirements. Learning from experienced professionals and industry experts will help you navigate potential challenges, mitigate risks, and maximize your returns.

One of the most effective ways to expand your knowledge is by joining real estate investment associations, local networking groups, or online communities. These platforms provide valuable opportunities to connect with like-minded individuals who have similar goals and aspirations. Engaging in conversations, sharing experiences, and seeking advice from seasoned investors can provide invaluable insights and help you make informed decisions.

Networking is not just limited to fellow investors; it also extends to professionals such as real estate agents, property managers, contractors, and lenders. Building relationships with these individuals can prove instrumental in finding the right deals, accessing financing options, and ensuring the smooth operation of your rental properties. Networking events, conferences, and industry-specific gatherings are excellent avenues to meet and connect with these key players.

Moreover, continuing education and networking go hand in hand. Attending educational seminars or workshops offers an opportunity to meet industry experts and connect with other participants. These events facilitate the exchange of ideas, experiences, and best practices, fostering a supportive network of professionals. By actively participating in discussions, asking questions, and sharing your expertise, you can establish yourself as a credible and knowledgeable investor within your niche.

Remember, the real estate market is highly competitive, and staying stagnant can hinder your progress. Embracing ongoing education and networking is key to remaining at the forefront of the industry. Continuously seeking knowledge and expanding your network will not only enhance your investment skills but also open doors to new opportunities that can propel your success as a single-family home rental property investor. So, invest in yourself and your network, and watch your portfolio flourish.

Appendix:

Sample Rental Property Analysis Spreadsheet

In the world of single-family home rental property investment, it is crucial to have a comprehensive understanding of the financial aspects involved. As an investor, house hunter, flipper, landlord, or property manager, you need a reliable tool to help you evaluate potential rental properties and make informed decisions. That's where the Sample Rental Property Analysis Spreadsheet comes into play.

This subchapter in "From House Hunter to Landlord: The Complete Handbook for Property Investment" is dedicated to introducing you to this invaluable resource. The Sample Rental Property Analysis Spreadsheet is a user-friendly, Excel-based tool designed to assist you in analyzing the financial feasibility of potential rental properties.

From House Hunter to Landlord:
The Complete Handbook for Property Investment in 2024

The spreadsheet enables you to input key data such as property purchase price, estimated rental income, operating expenses, financing terms, and more. It automatically calculates various financial metrics, allowing you to assess the property's potential cash flow, return on investment, and profitability. With this tool, you can quickly compare different properties and identify the most promising investment opportunities.

The Sample Rental Property Analysis Spreadsheet offers a range of features tailored to the specific needs of investors in single-family home rental properties. It includes sections for detailed income and expense projections, allowing you to forecast the property's financial performance over time. Additionally, it incorporates a mortgage calculator to help you determine the monthly mortgage payments and estimate the impact of different financing options on your cash flow.

Furthermore, the spreadsheet provides a comprehensive overview of the property's return on investment, including metrics such as cash-on-cash return, cap rate, and internal rate of return. These indicators allow you to assess the property's profitability and compare it to other investment opportunities.

By utilizing the Sample Rental Property Analysis Spreadsheet, you can streamline your property evaluation process and make well-informed decisions. Whether you are a seasoned investor or just starting out in the rental property market, this tool will save you time and effort while ensuring you have a clear understanding of the financial implications of each potential investment.

In conclusion, the Sample Rental Property Analysis Spreadsheet is an essential tool for anyone involved in single-family home rental property investment. It offers a user-friendly interface, comprehensive financial analysis, and valuable insights to help you make successful investment decisions. By incorporating this tool into your property evaluation process, you can confidently navigate the rental property market and maximize your returns.

Resources and Recommended Reading

As an investor, house hunter, flipper, landlord, or property manager interested in single-family home rental property investment, it is crucial to equip yourself with knowledge and resources to succeed in this competitive market. This subchapter provides a comprehensive list of valuable resources and recommended reading to help you navigate every stage of your property investment journey.

From House Hunter to Landlord:
The Complete Handbook for Property Investment in 2024

1. Real Estate Websites and Online Platforms:
Stay up-to-date with the latest market trends and property listings through popular real estate websites, such as Zillow, Trulia, Redfin, Realtor.com, and LoopNet. These platforms provide valuable insights into property values, rental rates, and investment opportunities in specific areas.

2. Books for Aspiring Investors:
For those new to property investment, "The Millionaire Real Estate Investor" by Gary Keller, "Rich Dad Poor Dad" by Robert Kiyosaki, and "The Book on Rental Property Investing" by Brandon Turner are highly recommended reads. These books offer practical advice, investment strategies, and inspirational stories from successful investors.

3. Property Financing and Taxation:
Understanding financing options and tax implications is crucial for any investor. Recommended books in this area include "The ABCs of Real Estate Investing" by Ken McElroy, "Loopholes of Real Estate" by Garrett Sutton, and "The Book on Tax Strategies for the Savvy Real Estate Investor" by Amanda Han and Matthew MacFarland.

4. Property Management and Landlording:
To manage your rental properties effectively, consider reading "The Landlord's Kit: A Complete Set of Ready-to-Use Forms, Letters, and Notices to Increase Profits, Take Control, and Eliminate the Hassle" by Jeffrey Taylor, "The Book on Managing Rental Properties" by Brandon Turner and Heather Turner, and "The Book on Negotiating Real Estate" by J Scott.

5. Real Estate Investing Podcasts:
Podcasts are a great way to learn on the go. Highly recommended podcasts in the real estate investing niche include "BiggerPockets Real Estate Podcast," "The Real Estate Guys Radio Show," and "The Best Passive Income Model" by Mark Podolsky.

6. Investment Networking:
Building a strong network is essential in the real estate industry. Attend local real estate investor meetups, join online forums, and participate in social media groups to connect with like-minded individuals and gain insights from experienced investors.

Remember, continuous learning and staying informed about current market trends are key to achieving success in single-family home rental property investment. Utilize these recommended resources and expand your knowledge base to make informed decisions, mitigate risks, and maximize your investment returns.

Glossary of Property Investment Terms

When diving into the world of single-family home rental property investment, it's important to familiarize yourself with the lingo that is commonly used in the industry. Understanding these terms will not only help you communicate effectively with professionals, but also enable you to make informed decisions as an investor, house hunter, flipper, landlord, or property manager. In this glossary, we have compiled key terms that you are likely to encounter on your property investment journey.

1. Cash Flow: The net income generated from a rental property after deducting all expenses, such as mortgage payments, maintenance, and property management fees.

2. Cap Rate (Capitalization Rate): A measure used to evaluate the potential return on investment by dividing the property's net operating income by its purchase price or current market value.

3. Appreciation: The increase in value of a property over time due to factors such as market demand, location, and improvements made.

4. Equity: The difference between the market value of a property and the outstanding balance on any mortgages or loans secured against it.

5. Gross Rental Yield: The annual rental income generated by a property divided by its purchase price or current market value, expressed as a percentage.

6. ROI (Return on Investment): A measure of the profitability of an investment, calculated by dividing the net profit by the initial investment and expressed as a percentage.

7. Rental Vacancy Rate: The percentage of time a rental property remains vacant within a given period, indicating its level of desirability and market demand.

8. Debt-to-Income Ratio: A calculation that compares an individual's monthly debt payments to their gross monthly income, used by lenders to assess borrowing capacity.

9. Lease Agreement: A legally binding contract between a landlord and a tenant that outlines the terms and conditions of the rental arrangement, including rental amount, lease duration, and rights and responsibilities of both parties.

10. Property Management: The professional service of overseeing the day-to-day operations and maintenance of a rental property on behalf of the owner, ensuring smooth tenancy and maximizing returns.

From House Hunter to Landlord:
The Complete Handbook for Property Investment in 2024

By familiarizing yourself with these property investment terms, you will be better equipped to navigate the complexities of the single-family home rental property market. Whether you are a seasoned investor, house hunter, flipper, landlord, or property manager, understanding these concepts will empower you to make informed decisions that can lead to success and profitability in the world of property investment. Remember, knowledge is power, and this glossary serves as a valuable tool to enhance your understanding of the terminology frequently used in the industry.

From House Hunter To Landlord:

The Complete Handbook for Property Investment for 2024

Benjamin has been in the real estate industry for 30 years. He has built homes, repaired, renovated and flipped properties. Benjamin has built a retirement portfolio of single family and multifamily properties. Let his experience guide you to a fulfilling retirement portfolio.